This book belongs to:

_____

_____

CROSS STITCH PATTERNS FROM 1730

Compiled by Angela M. Foster

You are welcome to use any of the <u>designs</u> in this book <u>to make things for</u> personal uses, charities, and selling.

ISBN 13 - 978-1519521507
ISBN 10 - 1519521502

Copyrighted © 2015 by Angela M. Foster
All Rights Reserved.

I dedicate this book to

all who love to use their hands

to make beautiful items.

7

9

11

13

14

15

17

20

21

22

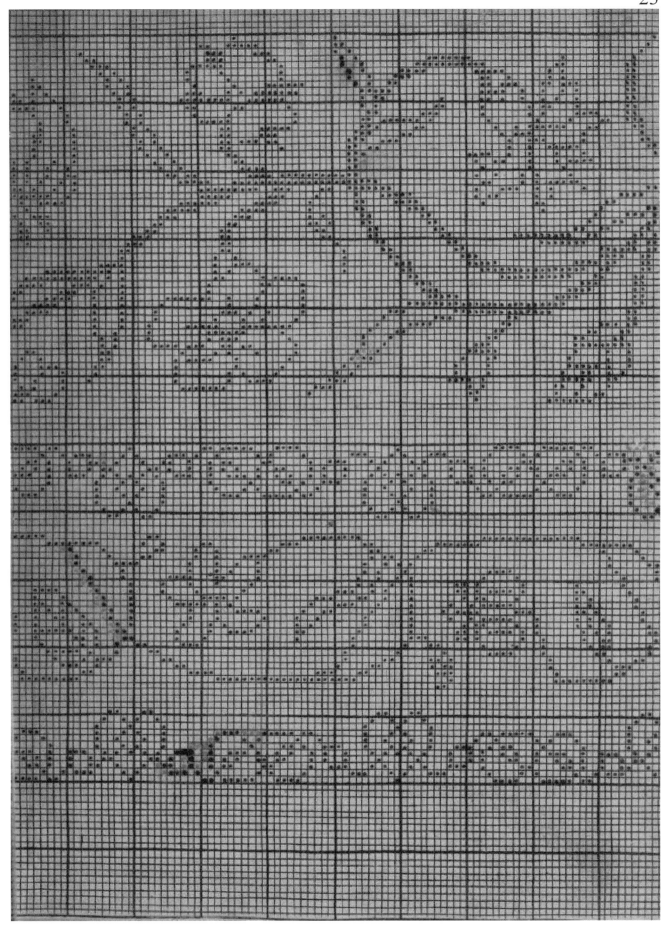

25

28

31

32

37

38

39

54

41

42

43

45

47

48

50

51

Made in United States
Orlando, FL
01 December 2023